Christmas in

Belgium

The Grand' Place is the site of many grand and
wonderful Belgian Christmas celebrations.

Christmas in

𝕭elgium

Christmas Around the World
from World Book

World Book, Inc.
a Scott Fetzer company

CHICAGO

Staff

President
  Robert C. Martin
Vice President and Publisher
  Michael Ross

Editorial

Managing Editor
  Maureen Mostyn Liebenson

Associate Editor
  Sharon R. Nowakowski

Writer
  Ellen Hughes

Manager, Cartographic Database
  Wayne K. Pichler

Permissions Editor
  Janet T. Peterson

Executive Director,
    Product Development
    and Research Services
  Paul Kobasa

Head, Indexing Services
  David Pofelski

Staff Indexer
  Tina Trettin

Art

Executive Director
  Roberta Dimmer

Art Director
  Wilma Stevens

Senior Designer
  Brenda B. Tropinski

Photography Manager
  Sandra Dyrlund

Photographs Editor
  Carol Parden

Production Assistant
  John Whitney

Product Production

Director, Manufacturing and Pre-Press
  Carma Fazio

Manufacturing Manager
  Barbara Podczerwinski

Senior Production Manager
  Madelyn Underwood

Print Promotional Manager
  Marco Morales

Proofreader
  Anne Dillon

Text Processing
  Gwendolyn Johnson

World Book wishes to thank the following individuals for their
contributions to **Christmas in Belgium:**
  Karen Zack Ingebretsen, Mary Kayaian, Irene Keller, Nancy Moroney
  and Mary Portier.

This book is dedicated to Irene Keller.

"The Simple Birth" from *The International Book of Christmas Carols,* by Walter
C. Ehret and George K. Evans.© 1963, 1980. Permission of Walter C. Ehret.
Every effort has been made to locate copyright holders of material in this volume.

World Book, Inc.
233 N. Michigan Avenue
Chicago, IL 60601

For information about other World Book publications,
visit our Web site http://www.worldbook.com or
call 1-800-WORLDBK (967-5325).
For information about sales to schools and libraries call:
1-800-975-3250 (United States); 1-800-837-5365 (Canada).

        Library of Congress Cataloging-in-Publication Data
Christmas in Belgium.
        p. cm. – (Christmas around the world from World Book)
    Summary: Describes the traditions and customs that are part of the celebration of
Christmas in Belgium as well as presenting crafts, recipes, and songs.
    Includes index.
    ISBN 0-7166-0864-2
    1. Christmas – Belgium – Juvenile literature. 2. Belgium – Social life and
customs – Juvenile literature. [1. Christmas – Belgium. 2. Belgium – Social life and
customs.] I. World Book, Inc. II. Series.

GT4987.53.C57 2002
394.2663 – dc21   2002068967

Printed in the United States of America
1 2 3 4 5 6 7 8 9 10 08 07 06 05 04 03 02

Contents

Christmas in Belgium is a truly special time. Its people and their history, as well as its culture and location, make Christmas in Belgium a mix of traditions. Its celebrations are among the best Europe has to offer.

Belgium is a small country in northwestern Europe. It is a little larger than the state of Maryland and has borders with four important nations—France, Germany, Luxembourg, and the Netherlands. A narrow strip of the North Sea separates Belgium from the United Kingdom. Its geographical position made Belgium an important industrial and trade center, but it has also made this small country into a battleground of warring nations. It suffered great destruction during World War I (1914-1918) and World War II (1939-1945).

Despite its small size, Belgium has a varied landscape. Dunes and beaches line its northern coast. Forest-covered hills cover much of the southeast. The central region has Belgium's best soil and is the site of many of the nation's largest cities, including Brussels and Liège. Belgium has mild winters with many snowfalls, but the snow melts quickly except in the Ardennes, a large region of forest-covered hills in southeastern Belgium.

Belgium has a rich architectural and artistic heritage. Stately cathedrals and churches built hundreds of years ago still stand in many towns and cities. Museums are filled with works by such outstanding Flemish artists as Jan van Eyck, Pieter Bruegel the Elder, and Peter Paul Rubens.

Belgium is one of the world's most densely populated countries. It is divided into two main ethnic groups—the Flemings and the

Snow doesn't stick around for very long in Belgium, but before it melts, it makes pretty wintry scenes like this one in Flanders.

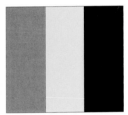

Belgium's coat of arms includes the national motto, *Union Provides Strength*, in French and Dutch. Belgium's flag was first used during the revolt against Austrian rule in 1789. It became the national flag in 1830.

Walloons. Most Flemings live in northern Belgium and speak Dutch. Most Walloons live in southern Belgium and speak French. Both Flemings and Walloons live in Brussels, the nation's capital. A group of German-speaking people lives in eastern Belgium. People wish *Merry Christmas* in many ways: in Dutch, *Vrolijke Kerstmis*; in French, *Joyeux Noel*; or German, *Frohliche Weihnachten!*

During most of its history, Belgium was a collection of cities and regions. Ancient Rome, Spain, Austria, France, and the Netherlands ruled the nation at different times. In 1830, Belgium won its independence from the Netherlands and became united as a state. The king is the head of state, and executive power lies in the hands

Introduction 7

Belgium lies in northwestern Europe. It borders the Netherlands, Germany, Luxembourg, France, and the North Sea. Belgium has three regions, which have a large degree of self-rule: Flanders, in the north; Wallonia, in the south; and the capital district of Brussels.

of the prime minister—the head of government—and the cabinet. Belgium has three economic regions and three separate language communities. These regions, which have a large degree of self-rule, are Flanders, in the north; Wallonia, in the south; and the capital district of Brussels. The three language communities are the Flemish community, which is made up of people who speak Dutch, the French-speaking community, and the German-speaking community.

The local government system includes the 11 provinces of Belgium and close to 600 *communes* (cities and towns). Dutch and French are both official languages in the country. The Belgian dialect of Dutch, previously called "Flemish," is now referred to as "Dutch."

Sometimes called "the capital of Europe," Brussels is now an international center of economic and political activity. The city is home to the headquarters of both the North Atlantic Treaty Organization (NATO) and the European Union, as well as many international companies. This mix of cultures and countries gives Brussels a cosmopolitan flavor. This mix also gives the capital a variety of traditions to choose from in presenting the richest Christmas offerings.

With its large buildings, cafés, and shops, Brussels appears to be a very modern city. However, many reminders of its past are found in the old section, called the lower city. At its heart stands the Grand' Place, or main square, which features a large marketplace bordered by elaborately decorated buildings constructed during the 1600's. This marketplace takes on a special glow at Christmas, when major squares and shops are illuminated by twinkling white lights, Nativity scenes are lovingly assembled, and holiday dinners are shared and enjoyed. Another highlight of the season in Belgium is the appearance of Saint Nicholas, who, like Santa Claus, is said to travel from rooftop to rooftop, bringing gifts for good children.

This scenic park in Bruges lies in the coastal lowlands of Belgium. Natural dunes, sea walls, and dikes protect these lands from flooding.

The Christmas Truce of 1914

Belgium's location has made it the scene of some of Europe's bloodiest battles. Sadly, a drive in the countryside here is a tour of battlefields and graveyards. However, one of Belgium's most moving true life Christmas stories comes from the battlefields of World War I (1914-1918).

Christmas comes to the trenches

The world war was only four months old, but it had already come to a standstill. Troops were dug into cold, muddy trenches only 60 to 100 yards apart along the Western front. The front stretched from the English Channel across Belgium and France to Switzerland. Neither side could advance. A soldier who dared to even lift his head above the top of a trench was likely to be shot in seconds by snipers.

A soldier's days were spent cowering in the trenches, bailing out floodwater, and desperately repairing mud walls as the freezing rain poured down. At night, the troops huddled together or stretched along the floor, fighting for sleep in the wet slime and the bitter cold. Trapped in their trenches, the soldiers on both sides were united in their common misery. They felt distant from the commanders, who had little or no experience of trench life.

As the first Christmas of the war approached, commanders on both sides worried about the possibility of a Christmas truce. They knew that soldiers who had made friends with each other might find it hard to start shooting again. Special orders came down the line. They said that there would be no Christmas truce. Anyone not fighting would be court-martialed.

Peace breaks out

According to eyewitness reports, strange lights appeared

During the 1914 Christmas truce, soldiers recovered and buried bodies from "no-man's land," the land between enemy lines.

along the German trench line on Christmas Eve. The British forces assumed the lights were some new kind of attack and prepared for the worst.

One look through binoculars changed everything, however. Those lights were on Christmas trees! The trees were aglow with candles and strings of lanterns.

Then, from the German trench came a rich chorus of voices singing the beautiful Christmas carol "Stille Nacht" ("Silent Night"). The British troops listened, then offered their own rendition of "The First Noel." Most important was the call repeated over and over up and down the line, "You don't shoot, we don't shoot."

One purpose of the truce was practical, but full of sorrow. Both sides wanted to bury the bodies of their dead friends. Crews from opposing armies worked alongside each other, finding and burying their own. In some places, the two sides even held joint prayer services and helped each other bury the dead. This genuine kindness in the midst of brutality was something the soldiers involved never forgot.

With the battleground cleared, men who were tired of fighting longed for friendly competition. Soon they started ball games along the lines.

Men met in the middle of the field to talk, share a cigarette, and walk together. Chatting wasn't easy though. As a rule, British soldiers spoke no German and only a few Germans could speak English. More often, a few phrases, lots of smiles, head nodding, handshakes, and holiday toasts were all that was needed to express friendship and goodwill.

Fighting resumes

The peace that broke out that Christmas was sporadic and spotty. In some places, it lasted through Christmas Eve and Christmas Day. In other areas, it stretched all the way through New Year's Day. Sometimes, the peace was suddenly cut short when a new commander or fresh troops arrived at the front.

In the book *Silent Night*, his historical account of the Christmas Truce of 1914, Stanley Weintraub sums up the tragedy that lay ahead: "On both sides in 1915 there would be more dead on any single day than yards gained in the entire year. And there would be four more years of attrition—not to determine who was right, but who was left." Never again during that long war was there a time of peace and mutual understanding as there was during that Christmas truce.

Starting
the Season

In preparation for the season, the medieval town of Bruges puts up lights in one of its historic markets.

While children in other countries wait for Santa Claus to bring them presents on Christmas Day, most Belgian children eagerly anticipate a visit from Saint Nicholas, their patron saint and main gift giver. He is called Saint *Nicolas* in French, Saint *Nikolaus* in German.

A visit from Belgium's bishop

Saint Nicholas takes special care of sailors, travelers, bakers, merchants, and, especially, children. He is their patron saint. Little is known about Saint Nicholas's life except that he was the bishop of Myra in Lycia, on the coast of Asia Minor. According to legend, Saint Nicholas was born in Lycia. Some legends say that he made a pilgrimage to Egypt and Palestine as a boy and that he was imprisoned by the Roman emperor Diocletian. He was freed by Constantine the Great. Legends also say that Nicholas attended the Council of Nicaea in A.D. 325.

Many miracles were credited to him too. Saint Nicholas is said to have died on December 6, in 343. That day became his feast day in the Roman Catholic Church. People attend church services that day and have special family dinners at home. Some people open gifts brought by Saint Nicholas. The gifts probably began with the legend that Saint Nicholas gave gold to each of three girls who did not have a dowry. In the past, brides gave their husbands money as a dowry.

In Belgium, Saint Nicholas first appears as early as a month before his special day. Unlike jolly, round Santa Claus, Saint Nicholas is tall and thin. He dresses like a bishop in a long flowing robe and carries a staff that looks like a shepherd's crook. According to Belgian tradition, he arrives from Spain on a boat! These days, he's just as likely to make his entrance marching in a parade, landing in a helicopter, or even riding in on a donkey. In some places, though, Saint Nicholas just magically appears.

In the city of Binche, Saint Nicholas parades through the streets during a welcoming festival held in his honor. As he passes along the parade route, he tosses oranges to the crowd. Sometimes he stops in shopping malls and supermarkets so that children can have their picture taken with him.

In the weeks leading up to Saint Nicholas Day, children in elementary schools learn holiday poems and songs to entertain the bishop when he arrives.

Many children in Belgium also write letters to Saint Nicholas. Of course, parents do the writing for very small children. Also, the Belgian postal service hires people to help Saint Nicholas answer all the letters. And each response includes a tasty treat from the kindly bishop.

On December 4, Saint Nicholas is in town again, this time to talk to the children and check up on their behavior. Have they been good? Have they obeyed their parents and teachers? Are they doing their best at school? Saint Nicholas has some serious questions to ask—and he wants answers!

The wrong answers could cause a lot of trouble though because *Zarte Piet* (Black Pete) travels with the kindly bishop. Black Pete is a dark-skinned, tough little fellow dressed in 16th-century-style clothing. Following a very old tradition, Black Pete is supposed to be a

> On the night of December 5 . . . children prepare for a nighttime visit from Saint Nicholas.

Saint Nicholas visits children on December 4 to ask them how they have been behaving. On the evening of December 5, excited children put out their shoes in anticipation of a nighttime visit from their patron saint. They hope to awake to shoes filled with goodies.

Moor from Spain—according to legend, a very dangerous person. He carries a large sack to put bad children in, and it is said that he hauls them back to Spain. He scares children by rolling his eyes, and may even brandish a whip, threatening to use it on bad children. On a lighter note, he often performs tricks and throws candy to children as he walks along.

One special night

On the night of December 5, Saint Nicholas Eve, children prepare for a nighttime visit from Saint Nicholas. Before going to bed, they put out *speculoos*—traditional Belgian Christmas cookies—and other Christmas treats, including a glass of beer for Saint Nicholas. Inside their shoes, they tuck a carrot or a turnip or some other vegetable for Saint Nicholas's horse, and sometimes hay or a little water too. Then they carefully set their shoes by the hearth or in front of a window.

Like Santa Claus, Saint Nicholas travels from rooftop to rooftop on this special night, leaving gifts for the children as he goes. Sometimes he simply tosses presents down the chimney. Saint Nicholas does not always travel in a sleigh pulled by reindeer, however. Instead, he may clop across the rooftops on a white horse or even on a donkey.

In the morning, children find the snacks gone. Inside the shoes and on the hearth, a good child will find an orange or a tangerine, along with some candies, nuts, and presents. A child who has been bad may find a whipping rod in the shoes or in a small basket just inside the front door. Saint Nicholas has also been known to leave an onion or a lump of coal. Whatever, the meaning is clear.

What kind of candies will the children find this Christmas? Chocolates shaped like the first letter of their name will surely be there, along with chocolates shaped like Saint Nicholas himself. There may be chocolate coins for good luck, and pink marzipan candies shaped like the Baby Jesus or like piglets. Seeing their presents, children will quickly run to the chimney and shout up, "Big thanks!"

> Saint Nicholas travels from rooftop to rooftop on this special night.

Saint Nicholas makes his rounds

On December 6, Saint Nicholas has many more visits to make. First, he is off to boarding schools. He must catch up with children he missed on his overnight ride. When he arrives, often riding his horse or donkey right into the school halls, the children are told to stand in line. Sometimes as many as 100 children are facing Saint Nicholas. Called to step forward one at a time, each child must face

Saint Nicholas as the headmaster solemnly reads a report about the child's behavior.

Of course, parents have secretly supplied information about each one of their children. This one was kind to the new baby sister, for example, and that one did not keep up with his schoolwork! Saint Nicholas praises the children for all the good they have done, and asks them to promise that any bad behavior will stop. Then chocolates and other candies are passed to everyone. Switches (thin, flexible rods or sticks) for whipping children, once a great threat, are seldom handed out today.

The heart of Brussels takes on a special glow at Christmas,

Later, Saint Nicholas may visit a city council meeting or the offices of a large company. The business of the day is then put aside, and Saint Nicholas is greeted with great courtesy. The secretary of state kisses his ring. So does the mayor. Grown-ups, too, may be rebuked for bad behavior or rewarded for good things they have done. And they can expect a little present from Saint Nicholas, such as a bag full of chocolates and speculoos shaped like the saint himself. His visits are taken seriously, and Saint Nicholas himself is always treated with great respect.

Decorations all around

Christmas decorations are going up everywhere—in homes, in restaurants, and in hotels. Holiday decorations in Belgium celebrate the beauty of the natural world during this season. Lush, green, fresh-scented Advent wreaths called *ker-stkrans* (Christmas rings) are hung on the doors and over the fireplaces on the days leading up to Christmas. Candles that represent the light of Christ are paired with evergreen branches, nuts, and pinecones, and trimmed with ribbon to decorate tabletops. Branches of greenery are draped over banisters and window frames.

Belgian houses are decked with ribbons, candles, lights, and garlands for the holiday season.

Advent is the season that marks the beginning of the Christian church year. It starts on the Sunday nearest Saint Andrew's Day (November 30), and it continues until Christmas Eve (December 24). The term comes from the Latin word *adventus*, which means coming or arrival. The season is one of preparation for the celebration of the feast of the Nativity of Jesus Christ on Christmas Day.

On the first Sunday, the family lights one candle and joins in prayer. They repeat this ceremony on each Sunday of Advent, lighting one additional candle each week. Three of the candles are purple, and the fourth one is pink. The pink candle is lit for the first time on the third Sunday, when people celebrate the beginning of the second half of Advent. On Christmas Day, all four candles may be replaced by four white ones, or a white candle may be added in the center. White symbolizes Jesus. Sometimes, people also use spe-

cial Advent calendars to keep track of the 24 days before Christmas. An Advent calendar has a colorful Christmas scene, and each date is printed on a flap. One flap is lifted daily to uncover a holiday picture or a Biblical verse.

Flowers are popular decorations and gifts at Christmas. In the small German-speaking section of Belgium, a person who gives a flower arrangement to a Belgian is sure to tuck in a little figure of a chimney sweep for good luck.

Christmas trees are more popular in Belgium every year. They are decorated with lights or small candles and with ornaments shaped like apples and other fruits, or like pinecones. Trees are also hung with speculoos. Little chocolate wreaths covered with *nonpareils* (chocolate drops sprinkled with sugar) are also tied onto the tree with red ribbons. Such edible decorations must be replenished during the season because children are allowed to take them from the tree and snack on them. Christmas trees may also be decorated with brightly colored ornaments and graceful garlands.

The custom of decorating houses with lights at Christmas is growing in Belgium. In many neighborhoods, local contests are inspiring more and more families to add Christmas lights to their houses and string them through their trees.

Typically, the shops in Belgium are closed on Sundays. But during the holidays, the shops stay open for business to accommodate busy holiday shoppers.

Delicate Designs

What is the white, delicate decoration on the Christmas tree? It's not snow. It's lovely, snowy-white Belgian lace.

The art of lacemaking developed in Europe during the 1500's. Belgium and Italy were the chief centers of early lacemaking. Today, the Kantcentrum (Lace Center) in Bruges is a foundation where the ancient art of lacemaking is passed on to the next generation. Lace of Bruges is famous around the world.

Handmade lace is classified according to the way it is made. The two main types are needlepoint lace and bobbin lace. Bobbin lace is a specialty of Bruge and is also very expensive. In making needlepoint lace, the lacemaker draws the design on parchment and sews it on a linen backing. Then he or she uses a needle and thread to fill in the pattern with embroidery stitches.

For bobbin lace, the design is drawn on parchment attached to a pillow. To make the lace, the lacemaker uses many bobbins (spools or reels) of thread. The thread is worked around small pins. The pins are stuck into the pillow along the lines of the design. Typically a lacemaker works with about 20 bobbins, but for complicated designs, more than 100 bobbins may be necessary. It could take three days to make a fine handkerchief medallion or handkerchief corner. Most handmade laces were named for the place where they were first made. Brussels is an outstanding needle lace, and Mechelen is a well-known bobbin lace.

Traditions are important during the holidays, and making fine lace by hand is one of Belgium's most famous. The woman above is making bobbin lace.

Shops throughout Belgium join in the Christmas celebration too. The legal ban on keeping a shop open on Sundays is lifted for the season, and shopkeepers fill their windows with Christmas decorations and gift suggestions. The town of Overijse in central Belgium awards a prize every Christmas to the shop with the best window decorations.

In Brussels, twinkling white lights illuminate the major squares and shopping streets during the holiday season. In the town of Spa in eastern Belgium, arrows point the way to shops, neighborhoods, and homes decked out and lit up for Christmas. People drive south from the city of Huy to the Château of Modave, a castle dating back to the 1200's. Glowing with Christmas lights, it looks like a fairy-tale castle.

Crèches

In French, it is called a *crèche*; in Dutch, it is a *kerststal*; in German, it is a *krippe*; and in English, a *crib*. The most beloved symbol of Christmas in Belgium is the Nativity scene, set in a stable and presenting the Baby Jesus nestled in a bed of straw in a manger. Mary and Joseph watch over him with the ox and donkey nearby offering their warmth, while shepherds watch their sheep outside. Three Wise Men lavishly dressed and jeweled arrive with their gifts, and one or more angels oversee it all.

In almost every public space of any size and in nearly every church and home in Belgium, Nativity scenes are set up at Christmas. Many are life-sized, and some include live animals—even live people. Others are tiny and precious, carved by famous artists, or placed near the altar of a church. Some are the loving handwork of children.

Traditional scenes of a stable in Bethlehem and a crèche set in a medieval German setting or a crumbling Belgian castle all have a place in Belgium's Christmas celebration. Often, the traditional Nativity scene includes several creative additions, such as Mexican donkeys, Russian dolls, and especially French *santons* (little saints). Some Nativity scenes feature carved figures that have been handed

Life-sized Nativity scenes appear throughout Belgium at Christmastime.

down in families for generations. The children of the family make others. Following a German custom, the family's Nativity scene is placed carefully under the Christmas tree. No Belgian city or village would be without a life-sized Nativity scene during the Christmas season, and some cities have a crèche on every city square. In Belgium's countryside, awe-inspiring Nativity scenes are simply placed at the edge of the roadway.

One of the most fantastic Nativity scenes of all has to be the illusion of a Nativity scene that is created by a light artist. The scene transforms Brussels's entire city center into a colorful fairy meadow with floating and grazing cows, donkeys, and sheep. A Christmas tree and a life-sized Nativity scene stand in the midst of all this. Every night, the amazing meadow becomes a starry night with countless tiny lights in the grass representing the stars in the sky on that long-ago night in Bethlehem.

Santons: Little saints from Provence

Many Belgian families follow the French tradition in the celebration of Christmas. They fill their Nativity scenes with santons from the French region of Provence. Santons are small figurines representing the Baby Jesus and all the people and animals present at the first Christmas, as well as a variety of local Provence folk. Today, an imaginative cast of characters from around the globe is often added. Santon makers offer hundreds of kinds of figurines representing people of all ages and occupations as well as animals. For example, there may be a baker, butcher, cheese maker, peddler, priest, and musician—each one appropriately dressed and carrying something that represents his or her occupation as a gift for the Baby Jesus.

Traditional santons are added to Nativity scenes. Each santon shows someone bringing a gift to the Baby Jesus, such as sticks, hens, knitted socks, fruit, and fish. The musician plays for the celebration.

Santons have been made in Provence since the early 1800's. They are sold at a Nativity fair in Marseilles as well as by individual santon makers in their own shops all the year around. The santon maker begins with a clay model of the figure. From this, he or she makes a two-part plaster of Paris mold. Then individual santons are "mass-produced" by being compressed in the mold by hand. Details are carved in the figure, which is then dried and baked in an oven.

Next comes the decoration that gives each santon its unique character. Details are added to the face and hands. Then comes the addition of hair, shirt, trousers or skirt, jacket, hat, shoes, other clothes and trappings, and a base. Parts of the finished santon, such as the basket the seamstress is carrying or the shoes of the little doctor, may be varnished to make them glossy and shiny, but the santon itself is not glossy and shiny. The traditional santon may stand 3 to 9 inches high.

Christmas Markets and City Celebrations

Strings of tiny twinkling lights and illuminated stars give a special glow to Christmas markets. Markets in city squares and downtown streets are the bustling center of life in Belgium, and at no time is that more apparent then during the holidays.

Markets galore

Nothing can match the fun and festive air of a Belgian Christmas market. The Belgian tradition of a Christmas market is reminiscent of fairs held throughout Europe during the Middle Ages. From early December through the holiday season, city and village squares in Belgium are filled with colorful little wooden stalls under strands of beautiful lights. They create a Christmas village filled with treasures. A huge selection of Christmas gifts and decorations awaits shoppers, plus many wonderful things to eat and drink.

In the city of Bruges in west Belgium, a Hobby Garden Christmas Happening gets the season started. This event begins on two weekends at the end

The colorful wooden stalls of the Christmas markets are filled with a huge selection of gift ideas and refreshments.

Belgians are sure to find an abundance of gifts, santons, and treats at this Christmas market in Antwerp, *right*. Many cities have more than one market.

Strolling through the magnificent Christmas market in Brussels's Grand' Place, Belgians take in a range of tastes, scents, and sights, *above*. Thousands of lights drape the historic square.

of November and is followed by the city's Christmas market on Market Square, complete with a giant ice-skating rink.

Many cities have more than one Christmas market. Most remarkable of all is the one held in Brussels's glorious Grand' Place, a lovely sight at any time of the year. Its large, cobbled square is bordered by the Gothic Hôtel de Ville, 39 baroque guild halls (meeting places of artisans or merchants, built in an ornate style), and the historic building called *Maison du Roi* (The King's House)

in French, which is also known as the *Broodhuis* (Bread House) in Dutch. Now, draped with thousands of Christmas lights and filled with brightly decorated wooden stalls and all the sounds and scents of Christmas, it is truly a wonder to behold. Strolling through the market, Belgians take in a range of Christmas tastes, scents, and sights. They can sip Scandinavian *glögg*, a hearty holiday drink. Or they can select Austrian wreaths for their doors or Irish greenery for their tables. Maybe they will choose santons from Provence, colorfully painted terra cotta animal figures from Mexico, or even handmade American Indian dolls to add to

After shopping and strolling through the market, these merrymakers enjoy a glass of cheer. Glögg is a popular and hearty holiday drink.

their Nativity scene at home. They may choose delicately woven straw and string ornaments from Finland or wooden nutcrackers from Germany. Perhaps they will buy an English plum pudding. Then, at the next row of wooden stalls, they may warm up with some hot fish stew, stir-fry vegetables, or Christmas beer. Along the way, shoppers find themselves entertained by a variety of musicians and also by painters who paint and sell their work on street corners. The holiday streets also provide a stage for Christmas plays, choirs, poetry readings, jugglers, and other performers.

Another highly celebrated and extravagant Christmas market is found on Market Square and Saint Lambert Square in the city of Liège. That city's Village de Noël presents a festival of Christmas music, crèches, and ornaments. More than 120 colorfully illuminated wooden chalets on the square offer hundreds of different Christmas delights. Handcrafts, crèche figurines, jewelry, Christmas wreaths, and other gifts can be bought while sampling Christmas beers and enjoying *glühwein* (mulled, or warm, spiced wine), *boudin* (sausages), oysters, and heavenly marzipan.

The Christmas market in Leuven, a city northeast of Brussels, is also a crowd pleaser. Its stands offer gifts, decorations, music, and Christmas lights and chocolates.

Sporty holidays

In Brussels, Liège, Antwerp, and other Belgian cities, the wonder of the Christmas market is paired with the fun of ice skating. Large ice rinks

One fun way Belgians burn off calories from delicious holiday sweets is by ice skating! The rink above sits amidst a festive market in the town square in Antwerp. The people at the right are skating in Flanders along one of Belgium's many frozen canals.

appear in city squares during the holiday season. Skating is perfect for working off all those doughnuts, waffles, and sausages—or for working up an appetite for more. Skaters may rent skates or bring their own. With skaters in mind, stalls in the Christmas markets sell warm sweaters, scarves, and gloves. And on Christmas afternoon in cities with canals, such as Ghent and Bruges, skaters race up and down the frozen waterways. Speed skaters carefully bypass the slower skaters, many of them grandparents and children just learning to skate.

Jogging is another popular way to burn off all those speculoos and marzipan piglets. Christmas jogging competitions are organized throughout Belgium, with prizes awarded.

At a Begijnhof

One of the season's most charming sights in Belgium is the Christmas celebration in one of the remaining age-old *Begijnhofs*, also called *Béguinages* (small towns within a town). In the 1100's and 1200's, the Crusades caused a shortage of men in Belgium and other European countries. A Belgian priest, concerned with the plight of Crusaders' widows and other young women with no men to marry, encouraged these women to form communities and live and work together. Generally, the women came from prosperous families who could afford to pay their entrance fee to the Begijnhof and help support them afterward. They had servants and lived comfortably, working and praying. They made lace, baked cookies, made sweets, and gave to the poor. While the women were religious, they were not nuns, and they could marry or leave the community at any time.

Some of these small enclosed worlds consisted simply of a few small houses surrounding a tiny courtyard. Others were larger and much more elaborate, with crisscrossing streets and as many as 1,000 residents. Usually, a Begijnhof contained a church, a hospital, and facilities for weaving, lacemaking, or other useful work.

> And on Christmas afternoon in cities with canals . . . skaters race up and down the frozen waterways.

During the Reformation, a religious movement of the 1500's that led to Protestantism, the Begijnhof movement continued to thrive in Catholic Belgium. Even now, Flanders has more than 20 Begijnhofs. Some Begijnhofs have been taken over by universities or sold to individual families. Visitors are welcome to tour the grounds at a Begijnhof, as long as they are quiet and respectful and leave before the gates close.

This stamp commemorates the small Flemish communities known as Begijnhofs.

At Christmas, some of the Begijnhofs become enchanting little worlds of sparkling celebration. They also turn on their famous cookie-making charm, baking traditional spicy speculoos as Christmas cookies for their guests. In Lier, the town's festive Christmas market is hosted in the very special atmosphere of the Begijnhof. At the Begijnhof in Turnhout, Christmas Eve is celebrated with the lighting of 1,000 candles. The Benedictine nuns at Bruges help organize religious services for Christmas Eve and Christmas Day.

Touring Nativity scenes

In Belgium, Nativity re-creators and their admirers are on the move all season. Walks or tours (*wandelingen* or *tochtjes*) to see Christmas sights—or even become a part of the celebration—are very much a part of the holiday festivities.

The Campine region located near Antwerp is famous for its giant-sized Christmas cribs. More than 300 Nativity scenes are found in marketplaces and churches, or simply at the side of a country road.

In 1957, the city of Turnhout in northern Belgium built a large Nativity scene on its marketplace. Since then, a growing number of cities have taken up the idea. Today, the countryside outside Antwerp at Christmas presents an inspiring array of full-sized

Bringing Christmas to Life

In Belgium, people's love for the Christmas story is seen in all kinds of plays, tableaus, and other colorful re-creations of the first Christmas.

Nativity plays especially are an age-old Christmas tradition here. In many villages in the Ardennes, two or three scenes of the Nativity story are acted out each year. Characters representing Mary, Joseph, the shepherds, and the three kings are not dressed in the simple clothing worn at that time in Bethlehem, however. Instead, they wear the kind of costumes that players wore when the tradition began in the 1500's. In Baasrode, the Christmas story is presented in 15 living scenes along a special route. Money collected from those who come to experience the story is donated to the poor.

The Nativity plays are sometimes "performed" by cut-out shadow puppets or regular puppets. The setting for the play may be a stable, a garden, or any public building in the village. In Verviers, visitors may view a Bethlehem reenactment presented by an order of Capuchin monks. Here, children standing underneath a stage operate mechanical puppets, re-creating events from the life of Jesus. A woman stands nearby, narrating the story.

Another very old tradition in Belgium is the living portrayal of the Three Wise Men. In small villages, it is customary for three popular men to be selected to play the wise men. Dressed in royal robes, carrying ceremonial staffs, and bearing gifts, the three kings walk from house to house. At each stop, they sing carols and are then rewarded with a small gift of food, which they are expected to eat on the spot! With this in mind, the Three Wise Men are often chosen for their size and their appetite as much as for their goodness or their singing voice. People often join the wise men on their walk, forming a growing parade of happy carolers as they go.

People in Mechelen create a living Nativity scene to celebrate Jesus's birthday.

A church in Antwerp displays a beautiful Nativity scene decorated with live plants and flowers.

Belgians admire a life-sized Nativity scene glistening in Grand' Place, Brussels.

Nativity scenes complete with beautiful lifelike statues, living animals, music, and lights. Each year, the Tourist Federation of the Province of Antwerp maps out four routes that people can travel to see some of the most beautiful cribs in the area.

In Melsele, a small town in the northwest near Sint-Niklaas, people are encouraged to walk or ride their bikes from one Nativity scene to another. In nearby Steendorp, Nativity scenes line the banks of the Schelde River. In Melle, a city just southeast of Gent, one can take a buggy ride, pedal a bike, or simply walk to enjoy Christmas stories, music, dance, decorations, and other holiday delights.

A band of musicians plays Christmas music in front of a life-sized crèche outside a church.

In Astene, a town near Deinze, people are invited to join in a mid-December Christmas walk. Starting at the church and carrying torches, the walkers are offered soup and rolls along the way. At their destination, mulled wine and a light show await.

In Antwerp, the annual Christmas walk on December 26 is an event no one wants to miss. The churches present artwork and sacred objects with the Nativity as their theme. In addition, several convents and privately owned mansions open their doors to visitors to share holiday cheer. While walking through the city, people can take in the bright Christmas lights of the city center and view Nativity scenes on many city squares.

In Brussels, thousands of people line up to view the immense Russian Nativity scene on display at the Basilica of Koekelberg. With its many figures, the scene spreads out over thousands of feet around the basilica. While viewing the Nativity scene, visitors enjoy a concert of Russian music.

In the far northwestern village of De Klinge, the Nativity scene is the center of Christmas activity, including performances by the Royal Fanfare St. Celicia, a youth choir, and an adult choir. In Manderfeld, a small German-speaking town in eastern Belgium, the Krippana Museum displays Christmas cribs from around the world.

In the northern city of Brasschaat, an exhibit of international crèches is joined by a group of Nativity scenes created by local schools, local artists, and hobbyists. An annual favorite is the display of wax figurines in the Nativity scene created by the Convent of the Clarissen nuns. In Bilzen, a city in northeastern Belgium, the live Nativity scene at the castle of Alden Biesen offers something extra— singing shepherds!

Bokrijk offers people the opportunity to immerse themselves in the fun of theater during the week between Christmas and New Year's.

Christmas performances

Belgians love good music. This is never more obvious than during Advent, when a long list of concerts is offered in many cities. The performances of regional choirs and musical societies are special here. One can attend performances by local school choirs, professional all-boy choirs, church choirs, and world-renowned adult choirs. Most churches publish a schedule of musical events during the holidays.

In Waterloo, people gather at Saint Joseph's Church for a concert that includes performances by more than 20 individual choirs. One choir sure to be on the program is Les Pastoreux, an all-male group admired throughout Europe.

Theater is also part of the celebration. Classic Christmas productions vie for attention with modern plays and musicals and amateur offerings. The annual Midwinter Event that is hosted by the Bokrijk

Openluchtmuseum (Open-air museum), near Genk, offers people the opportunity to immerse themselves in the fun of theater during the week between Christmas and New Year's. Thousands come to town each year to enjoy this unusual event. The open-air museum itself becomes one big theater, presenting numerous plays. There are demonstrations by crafts people and theater companies, and auditions for actors. For children of all ages, there are light shows, storytelling, and an exhibit of ice sculptures.

The Bokrijk Open-air Museum dazzles thousands of people each year with its spectacular holiday light show and other theatrical productions.

Holiday Traditions and Superstitions

The charm and tradition of Belgium has lasted for generations. This scenic depiction of the outskirts of Antwerp is by the Flemish painter Sebastian Vrancxs, who lived from 1573 to 1647.

With the mix of cultures in Belgium, there are many traditions—some religious, and others just for fun. And there are many superstitions too—some now abandoned, but others still followed today.

Here comes Santa!

Clearly, Saint Nicholas is very much the star of the season in Belgium. However, the international flavor of Belgium's Christmas markets in recent years means that a jolly elf in a red suit participates, too! Yes, you'll find Santa Claus himself, known as the *Kerstman* in Dutch, putting in many appearances during the holiday season in Belgium.

In the town of Brakel in central Belgium, Santa Claus arrives in a handsome horse-drawn carriage. In the city of Genk in the northeast, he rides in on his sleigh. But in the city of Herentals in the north, he strolls around on foot, checking out ice sculptures and sampling local goodies at the Christmas fair.

In Leuven, and in the little town of Wieze, in the northwest, Santa offers gifts and sweets to children at his own little house. In the city of

Though Saint Nicholas is the star of the season, much to the delight of Belgian children, Kerstman (Santa Claus) brings good tidings in December as well.

Tessenderlo in the north, the Christmas market features multiple Santa Clauses accompanied by fire-eaters.

Mass of Gold, Mass of Water

At 6 A.M. on the Wednesday before Christmas in the city of Namur in central Belgium, it is a long-standing tradition to celebrate the Mass of the Dawn. This special service blesses those who travel in their work, including salesmen, messengers, and ferrymen. At first, it was called the Mass of Gold because the sacred text for the service began with those words. Later, the name was changed to the Mass of Water. This may have been due to the great appeal that the Mass had for ferrymen. Large numbers of ferrymen came to the services every year because they believed the Mass helped protect them from drowning. At Mass, according to legend, the first shepherd to present himself will have the most beautiful lambs in the entire region.

Pilgrimage to the Christ of Tancrémont

The days leading up to Christmas also hold a special magic for some young ladies. According to tradition, girls who want to find husbands make a pilgrimage to the Christ of Tancrémont just before Christmas. The Christ of Tancrémont is a crucifix that was built along the road between Leuven, a small town southeast of Liège, and Pepínster to the northeast. This shrine is unusual because it presents Jesus wearing a long tunic. After their prayers, the girls usually have a small meal inside the iron fence of the roadside shrine before heading home.

Midnight Mass

In Belgium, which is an almost entirely Roman Catholic country, elaborate and beautiful religious services are the main events at Christmas. Most people attend Midnight Mass on Christmas Eve, and many return for church services on Christmas Day.

On Christmas Eve, a wonderful feeling of community and spiritual closeness exists among neighbors and among strangers, too. In cities and small villages, people walk to church on that evening, joining in the passing procession. What begins as a few people may number in the hundreds by the time they reach the doors of the church on Christmas Eve. The Midnight Mass service is typically candlelit and the church is filled with beautiful music.

In Beveren, in far western Belgium, Christmas is welcomed with Christmas music and a living Nativity scene in front of the church. After Midnight Mass, the Christ Child is symbolically baptized before the congregation. The night ends with friends and family sharing a glass of glühwein around a roaring bonfire on the village square.

Most Belgians attend an elaborate and beautiful Midnight Mass on Christmas Eve. Music fills the church, which is typically candlelit.

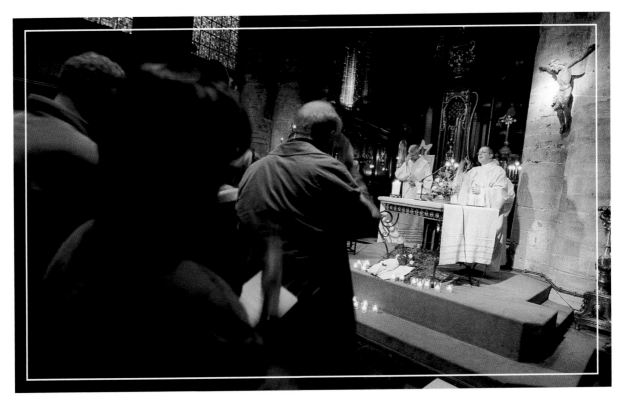

The game of trairies

Trairies is a Christmas card game that has been enjoyed throughout Belgium for generations. The players are not in the game to win money, though. They're hoping to win a sweet bread shaped like the Baby Jesus. In the past, trairies was a game for men only, and it was played in the back rooms of bakeries. Today, groups of players—males and females of all ages—play trairies in cafés and bakeries.

In keeping with tradition, after Midnight Mass, friends meet in the center of their village and then head to the bakery. Each person gives some money to the *boulangère* (baker) or his or her spouse. When enough has been collected, the game begins.

The group picks a leader to start the game. He or she shuffles the cards and deals out one card per player. The one with the highest card of the same color as the dealer's card is the first winner, and he or she receives the biggest prize. After each round of the game, another prize is given out.

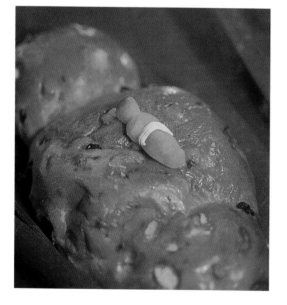

A candy figure in the shape of the Baby Jesus sits gently atop the traditional Christmas sweet bread called cougnou, which is also in the shape of the Baby Jesus. It is a prize for a winner of the Christmas game trairies.

The traditional prizes are five *cougnous*—each one smaller than the next. A cougnou is a sweet Christmas bread made with raisins and shaped like the Baby Jesus wrapped tightly in thin blankets called swaddling clothes. In the center of each little cake is a small terra cotta decoration called a *Rond de Cougnole*, or sometimes a little candy figure of the Baby Jesus. First prize in a game of trairies is a cougnou that weighs about 2 pounds. The smallest prize is a cougnou that weighs only 3 ½ ounces.

Players know trairies is a game of chance, not a game of strategy. Those who don't win a cougnou in the first game will try their luck in another game or at another bakery. Players enjoy going from bakery to café to bakery, carrying bags full of cougnous and showing off their prizes.

The baker's spouse will keep the bakery open for hours, knowing that the not-so-lucky will be back to buy cougnous when the games are over. Nothing tastes better on Christmas morning than a cup of hot chocolate or coffee and a cougnou. Many families can't wait for morning. Some parents wake their children as soon as the cougnous arrive and they all start Christmas by sharing this special treat in the wee hours.

At the Dieudonné boulangèrie in Andenne, where the game has been played at Christmas for generations, men line up on the street for hours, waiting for their chance to enter the back room. All is fine until about 3:30 A.M. Then it's time for the baker to start baking bread for the morning, and the games must end!

Celebrating in the Ardennes

At Christmas, many Brussels residents make an annual tradition of getting away for a few days, or just for an evening, to one of the beautiful country inns in the Ardennes. There, they take in the lovely scenery of forests and fields and enjoy the delights of the Christmas table. The menu often lists trout

A gentle Christmas snow makes for a beautiful cross-country-skiing trek in the Ardennes region of Belgium.

fresh from a nearby stream, rabbit, and juicy *sangliers* (wild boar). The inns of the Ardennes are also known for serving the finest champagne and wine, as well as many of Belgium's gourmet beers.

Gift-giving

Christmas Eve or Christmas Day dinner is the time for family gift-giving. If there is a Christmas tree, the presents are likely to be placed under its branches until the time comes to open them. Santa Claus, called the *Kerstman* in Dutch, is not really part of the Belgian tradition. Santa Claus was not even known in this country until about the 1960's. Thanks to advertising and television, however, he is now a well-known figure. French and Protestant children know the Christmas Eve visitor who leaves gifts under the tree as Saint Nicholas or *Père Noël* (Father Christmas). German-speaking Belgian children generally receive a present from Saint Nicholas on his feast day early in December, but many also receive a welcome visit from a gift-bearing *Christkindl* (Christ Child) on Christmas Eve.

During the holidays, traditions are passed from one generation to the next. Reading Christmas stories, exchanging presents, baking, and feasting are just a few of the ways people enjoy the season together.

Symbols from long ago

Christmas and New Year were once holidays that provided many ways to find out your luck—good or bad—or to set the stage for a better year ahead. Some beliefs and rituals are still used today. Others can be glimpsed behind present Christmas customs. The following customs were among the most widely practiced in Belgium in the past.

The Christmas candle—traditionally made of pure beeswax—was a beautiful religious symbol said to represent Jesus. At midnight on Christmas Eve, families would light one tall candle in their house to celebrate the birth of the Baby Jesus. This candle then took on a power of its own. It could be used at other times of the year, for example, to stop a thunderstorm. It was also thought that if the candle went out during the night, it meant that someone in the house would die. And, placed in the hand of a person "in the agony of death," the candle was said to help rid the body of evil spirits.

Many Christmas customs in Belgium centered around the belief that the infant Jesus blessed anything left out in the open on Christmas Eve. Bread sprinkled with salt was often placed on an outside windowsill overnight. This bread ensured plenty of food for the family in the year ahead. On Christmas Eve, farmers often poured water in a circle all around fields where crops were grown to protect the crops from field mice, disease, and insects.

Farmers especially had good reason to wonder how the weather would be in the year to come. According to old Belgian customs of the season, Christmas allowed farmers to get some answers! A "*claire*," starry night on Christmas Eve was thought to predict a "somber" or dark barn. That meant a barn filled with crops at the time of the harvest.

According to legend, what you do and don't do at Christmas can bring you luck . . .

To learn the temperature for the new year, a person could float 12 nutshells in a basin of water, each shell containing a tiny lighted candle. For every shell that capsized and doused its light, the farmer could expect one humid month in the next year.

In the province of Luxembourg, a similar custom used onions. First, 12 onion slices were spread out and sprinkled with coarse salt. The onion rings that caused the salt to melt represented rainy months.

Other people in Belgium believed that all you needed to do was keep one eye on the calendar and one eye on the sky. The weather for each of the 12 months ahead would be the same as the weather on each of the 12 nights after Christmas.

According to legend, what you do and what you don't do at Christmas can bring you luck—or take it away. First, be careful when and where you work. It is best not to work at all on Christmas Day. One old saying decrees that "he who washes his laundry on Christmas prepares his shroud." In Herve, however, an exception is made for washerwomen.

Also, it's a good idea to tie a piece of straw around the trunk of your fruit trees at Christmastime. This will protect them from late frost and insects. A peasant who gently notches the trunk of his fruit tree now will have an abundance of fruit in spring.

Though the growing season is far off, consider planting something now. Whatever you plant in the snow is sure to grow, according to an ancient Belgian custom. Also be sure to mark the day of the week that Christmas falls on. When it is time to plant crops, this day is your best bet. Crops that are put into the ground on that day will grow in abundance.

If family members are away from home on Christmas Eve, place an onion on the family altar for each absent person, and write their name on the onion. If the onion sprouts, the absent person will remain in good health.

> On Christmas Eve, place an onion on the altar for each absent person . . . .

On Christmas Eve, a young single girl should put an apple branch and a currant branch in a vase. If the branches bloom during Christmas, the girl can expect to be married within the next year!

A newly married couple should throw nutshells onto the hearth. If the shells burn up quietly, the marriage will be peaceful. If the shells pop and crack, though, there will be plenty of "noise" in the marriage, too.

Being born on Christmas Eve is a very good thing, especially if the baby is redheaded as the Belgians believed Jesus was. A Christmas Eve baby was thought to be a prophet—someone who has the power to interpret great mysteries.

The animals

In the past, animals were a major part of Christmas activity on a Belgian farm. According to tradition, the supporting role that animals played in the Bethlehem stable on that first Christmas Eve earned farm animals permanent respect during this holy holiday. Some farmers would tell their farmhands not to change the straw in the stables that night or disturb the straw in any other way. More commonly, farmers would make a very big production of cleaning the stables that night.

On Christmas Eve day, the animals were let out to wander while the stalls were emptied and cleaned. When the animals returned, they found piles of clean hay beneath their feet and twice as much food in the manger. They, too, were being invited to celebrate the birth of Jesus with a joyous feast. The cattle and the donkeys would kneel down at midnight on Christmas Eve, "as did their glorious ancestors before the crèche," according to Belgian tradition. Some people even believed the donkey spoke. No one can say if any of this really happened, of course, because no one saw it. The tradition also says that anyone who dared to witness all this would be hit by sudden death.

On Christmas Eve, some farmers would let the animals out of the barn and then clean it top to bottom. When the animals returned, there would be fresh piles of hay and twice as much food.

Belgian farmers brought their sheep into the barn for safekeeping that night—being careful not to mention the wolf! If you talked about a wolf on Christmas Eve, a lamb would disappear.

To protect their chickens, the farmers would spread the broth from a blood sausage around the outside of the chicken coop. They also gave the chickens a meal of oats. This was intended to protect them from harm—and also to keep them from laying eggs in the neighbor's yard!

Farmers often placed pinches of ashes from the Bûche de Noël at the four corners of a storage container. This was believed to help avert bad luck.

Farmers also placed armfuls of hay in front of their doors on Christmas Eve night. In the morning, they spread this blessed hay around the barn floor to protect the barn and the animals from violent weather and other natural disasters throughout the coming year.

Tastes of the Season

Belgium has plenty to offer every sweet tooth, such as speculoos, spice cookies, and waffles!

Christmas in Belgium is a time for family and friends to join together over great holiday dinners. Cities and villages all around Belgium have their own special holiday dinner traditions that add magic and meaning to the season.

Speculoos

The days leading up to Christmas are filled with anticipation. Wonderful Belgian spice cookies, called speculoos, are baked in nearly every kitchen and sold in nearly every bakery. These tasty gingerbread cookies get their flavor from a combination of cinnamon, ginger, and cloves. They are also a Christmas favorite in Germany, Austria, and the Netherlands. In those countries, the cookies are called *speculaas*.

Whatever their name, these cookies spell Christmas to children in Belgium. The flat speculoos are usually cut or pressed into shapes and sometimes decorated with melted white chocolate and red sugar sprinkles. Speculoos come in all sizes—from bite-sized morsels to cookies as big as a 5-year-old child. Many speculoos will be tied with ribbons and hung on the Christmas tree.

Dinnertime

Christmas dinner may be enjoyed either before or after Midnight Mass or even on Christmas Day. Dinner on Christmas Day in Belgium typically starts at noon and, in European fashion, stretches on for hours, lasting easily until 4 P.M. In the past, people usually fasted hours before taking Communion at church. Today, the tradition is more relaxed, and many families plan to have their dinner later in the evening, just before going to church. Many young families celebrate with all their relatives by having Christmas dinner on Christmas Eve with one side of their family and on Christmas Day with the other side.

An elaborate Christmas meal may be served late Christmas Eve or Christmas Day. Salmon or some other seafood is almost always on the menu.

French traditions

In French-speaking Belgium, as in France, Christmas dinner is the center of Christmas celebrations and a very important occasion to share with family. Following the festive French supper tradition of *Le réveillon*, some families in Belgium complete all dinner preparations on Christmas Eve day, and then wait until after Midnight Mass to eat. They begin their Christmas festive feast in the wee hours of Christmas morning. A meal with up to 15 courses could stretch out all through the night, of course, leaving sleepless parents to deal with children who rise at dawn!

All around French-speaking Wallonia, one lovely feature of the typical Christmas dinner celebration is singing. Everyone joins in. The family has many old Walloon Christmas carols to choose from,

all known for their simplicity and their lovely melodies. In the town of Bra, it is customary for families to prepare food from the réveillon table to take to the cemetery. By singing carols at the cemetery and leaving some Christmas treats on the graves of deceased relatives, the people express their devotion and welcome their loved ones to their Christmas feast.

The holiday menu

Whenever it is held, the Belgian family's Christmas feast is an amazing, multi-course affair. Starting with champagne and heading through course after course of the most delicious gourmet offerings, it is a Christmas dinner unmatched anywhere.

Belgians love food—and for good reason. Cooking in Belgium is a genuine labor of love. When a Belgian hostess or waiter asks you *"C'était suffisant?"* ("Did you get enough?"), you are still tempted to say no because the selection of appetizers, entrees, vegetables, desserts, and drinks is so incredible.

Christmas dinner traditionally starts with champagne and appetizers. Then comes a "starter" course, possibly seafood, followed by many other wonderful choices. Stuffed roast turkey is typically the main dish today, but it could also be a game bird or *venison* (deer meat).

There likely will be oysters, lobster, salmon, *bisque de homard* (crayfish soup), *pâté de foie gras* (a paste made from goose liver), and, sometimes, caviar. Seafood is almost always included in this extravagant meal.

A dish sure to be part of the celebration is *aardappel kroketjes* (fried potato croquettes). Other classic Christmas dishes are celery root and potato purée, baked apples filled with berries, or pears poached in spiced red wine.

Belgians are not interested in serving the same traditional Christmas dinner year after year, though. The joy of cooking wins out over tradition. Guests would be disappointed if Christmas dinner didn't include some delightful surprises.

> Cooking in Belgium is a genuine labor of love.

Christmas breads

The customary Belgian Christmas sweet bread, won in a game or bought at a bakery, comes in different shapes at different times and places. First, everywhere in Belgium and France there is the *brioche*, a sweet eggbread or small cake with a small ball-shaped dough on top. In Andenne, this has been transformed into the *cougnou*, a little cake or bread made with raisins and sugar in the shape of the Baby Jesus. In the province of Namur, it's *cougnioles*. In the province of Hainaut, it's *kenioles*. In other places, they are called *quéniole* or *cuniole*, from a Latin word meaning cradle or swaddling clothes. Whatever the name, though, it tastes like Christmas in Belgium.

In the town of Ath, the local version of a cougnou is called a *couque du petit Jésus*. In Huy, the bread is not shaped like the Baby Jesus, but like a little man.

The traditional Christmas meal in Belgium ends with the Bûche de Noël . . .

Tasty boukètes

In Liège at Christmas, hosts delight their guests with an offering of *boukètes*. These are buckwheat *crepes* (thin pancakes) that have been fried in a pan with butter, raisins, and apple rings, and then sprinkled with brown or white sugar. In Herve, the boukètes are usually served with hot wine and pear and apple syrup.

These traditional Christmas treats are also sold by street vendors at certain times of the year. Children sometimes call boukètes "spit crepes" because street vendors often spit on their griddle to see if it is hot enough to make crepes, just as women sometimes spit on an iron to test its temperature.

In the region of Tienen near Leuven, the traditional Christmas pastry, called a *toteman*, is made with raisins and sugar and shaped like a child.

Bûche de Noël

The traditional Christmas meal in Belgium ends with the *Bûche de Noël*, a cream-filled chocolate cake or ice-cream cake shaped like a log and topped with snowy icing. This is the delicious modern version of an age-old French Christmas custom, the original Bûche de Noël (Christmas log).

In the past, the head of the house would go to church on Christmas Eve to get burning embers. The embers were used to start a new fire in the family hearth. He then placed three enormous logs in the fireplace, using the embers to light them. These logs heated the house and provided a blessed new fire to celebrate Christmas and start the year off right. In addition, the Bûche de Noël was used to start the Feast of Hot Wine. The hostess poured wine into a copper pot and heated it over the Bûche de Noël, adding several cinnamon sticks and three cloves. When the wine was boiling, the family members and guests waited silently while the host sprinkled the hot wine over the cinder of the fire in the sign of the cross. Then he filled the family's best porcelain cups and served the mulled wine to his guests.

Even after feasting for hours, who could pass up a taste of delicious Bûche de Noël?

Sacrificing the pig

In the city of Martilly in southern Belgium, an ancient ritual called for the "sacrifice" of a pig at Christmas. The pork was then distributed, usually in the form of *boudin* (sausages), to all the town's families. The best part was always saved for the parish priest.

In Liège today, women follow a similar tradition by boiling both white and red boudin in pig blood to serve at Christmas. In Namur, it wouldn't be Christmas without *snikèyes*, the tasty end pieces of pork ribs, lightly salted and braised, and served with potatoes.

A Sweet Celebration

Skip the sugarplums. At Christmas in Belgium, children and adults alike are sure to have visions of exquisite little chocolates dancing in their heads—and soon to be melting in their mouths.

Melts in your mouth

Belgian chocolates are said to be the finest in the world. That reputation has been earned through uncompromising insistence on quality. Belgian chocolatiers use only the finest chocolate, the freshest cream fillings, and the most exacting production techniques—all in pursuit of the perfect praline. *Praline* is the Belgian name for a very important Belgian creation—the hard chocolate shell that holds, or, as chocolatiers prefer to say, "enrobes," a cream filling. The French call it a chocolate bouchée, a bonbon, or simply a chocolate. All over the world, people know it as the fanciest kind of chocolate confection, however it was the Belgians who invented the praline. Pralines and other chocolate confections are made according to closely guarded family recipes. But we do know that companies in other countries save time and money by using vegetable fats instead of cocoa butter. But in Belgium, chocolate companies insist on pure cocoa butter. Pure cocoa butter has a wonderful cooling effect as it melts in your mouth.

Pretty packages

Fine chocolates are the perfect gift for the young and old, and the chocolatiers of Belgium make sure that everyone unwraps something delightful. Neuhaus is one of the finest names in Belgian chocolate. In 1857, Jean Neuhaus set up shop at 27 Galerie de la Reine in Brussels. Neuhaus's original store was more of a pharmacy than a sweet shop. Neuhaus made and sold sweet cough drops, licorice sticks for stomach problems, and bars of bitter chocolate. Eventually, the pharmaceutical line was replaced with caramels, fruit jellies, and chocolates. In 1912, Jean Neuhaus, Jr., the founder's grandson, created the praline, a bite-sized, cream-filled chocolate. Soon after that, Jean and his wife, Louise Agostini, invented something that revolutionized the chocolate world—a beautiful box, called a *ballotin*, to safely transport and store delicate confections. The boxes are tied up with a traditional gold and green ribbon, which was first designed to demonstrate young Jean Neuhaus's respect for Napoleon Bonaparte, the famous French emperor and general.

Christmas delights

Belgian chocolatiers offer a selection of classic holiday chocolates and molded designs to add to the Christmas and New Year's celebrations. There are chocolate "logs," shaped like the traditional Bûche de Noël, filled with candies and topped with a holiday bow; chocolate shoes loaded with treats; and molded chocolate figurines.

Leonidas, another top chocolatier, was founded in Brussels in 1913. Along with figurines of Saint Nicholas and Père Noël in dark, milk, and ivory chocolate, Leonidas offers cats, dogs, pigs, squirrels, cars, pelicans, bears, soccer players, and girls shaped in

CHOCOLATIER

People in Belgium and around the world enjoy receiving melt-in-your-mouth Christmas treats from Belgium's famous chocolatiers.

ply delicious chocolates to businesses located in Brussels. Joseph Draps named the brand Godiva after a legendary English woman who was elegant, rich, sensual, and daring. Draps felt his chocolates expressed those qualities. Godiva offers such delights of the season as a Christmas tree enclosing a ganache (a mixture of chocolate and heavy cream) flavored with mulled wine, cinnamon, nutmeg, and orange peel, and a Christmas boot made of milk chocolate and trimmed with marzipan "fur." A small Christmas log of dark chocolate with hints of orange, rum, and cinnamon suits the season.

For the New Year's celebration, Belgians are sure to pick up champagne corks made of chocolate and filled with champagne or rum, or a Christmas ball made of half dark and half white chocolate.

chocolate to delight all the children on your list. In addition, apples, pears, carrots, turnips, and other fruits and vegetables made of marzipan are perfect table decorations.

Who wouldn't love opening Godiva's familiar golden box with special Christmas bows and flourishes on top? Godiva, a fine chocolate name and a taste familiar to people around the world, is another Belgium chocolatier gem. The Draps family opened a chocolate workshop in 1926 to sup-

From
Christmas
into the
New Year

 he time from Christmas to the start of the New Year is a busy one for the people of Belgium. Whether they are attending the horse show, celebrating romance, enjoying a brisk swim, or dismantling their Christmas tree, there is much to do.

Lovers' Day

In the far south of Wallonia, the day after Christmas is called Lovers' Day, a custom that goes back to the Middle Ages. People who were married during the year stroll through the streets together in a procession. The walk leads to an eating contest—a friendly competition suggesting that couples should enjoy the good things in life.

Fair of the Lovers, Fair of the Nuts

On one special day late in December, nuts are thrown to the children of Bastogne from the balcony of the city's Hotel du Ville. The Fair of the Nuts traditionally marked the end of the agricultural year, the time when farmers rehired their servants, field hands, cowboys, and shepherds for another year's work. With money in their pockets and the promise of work in the year ahead, the

A grand display of fireworks helps ring in the new year in Brussels.

After Christmas, even Santa Claus arrives at the world-famous Horse Show in Mechelen, *right*, to watch the jumping competitions, *far right*, and more.

laborers headed out to have a good time. Traditionally, young men would offer fruits and nuts to the girls they wanted to marry, giving rise to the name Fair of the Lovers or the Fair of the Nuts.

The horse show

The day after Christmas also is the start of the world-famous Flanders-European Christmas Horse Show in Mechelen. This international horse-jumping competition draws riders from around the globe and a crowd of 50,000 spectators. Here, along with the featured jumping contest, visitors can observe competitions in

dressage, an auction of top racehorses, demonstrations with Brabant draft horses, and mini-steeplechases for ponies—and very young riders! Then, participants and spectators alike can stroll through a large commercial fair offering riders equipment and equestrian

articles of nearly every description. This much-anticipated annual event is always held during the week between Christmas and New Year's. The horse shows and competitions are televised.

New Year's celebrations

In Belgium, New Year's Eve is a night for families and friends to celebrate at private parties, large and small. Staying up together to see the new year in, they dance and dine on gourmet treats. At the stroke of midnight, there are kisses and champagne toasts all around.

In the German-speaking section of Belgium, a big New Year's Eve dinner is the custom. This is likely to be served buffet-style, with the most luxurious foods being offered. There is bound to be lobster, all kinds of seafood, and pâté de foie gras, plus plenty of fine wine and champagne.

Fireworks are increasingly popular as a flashy end-of-year display in Belgium. There may be no throng of people counting down the minutes to midnight and waiting for the ball to drop, as there is in New York City's Times Square. Instead, fireworks make a colorful backdrop for the dinners, parties, and outings with friends and family that New Year's Eve is all about in Belgium.

Beautiful fireworks light up the night over Place de l'Albertine in Brussels.

The settings for the fireworks here can be pretty dramatic themselves. In Westende and Middlekerke and in Ostend, fireworks light up the beaches of the North Sea on New Year's Eve. The fireworks here are sometimes called a Sylvester Night celebration, in honor of an old, bearded character who, according to German/Austrian tradition, represented the old year passing.

Brussels boasts that its year-end fireworks and light show in Albertina Park are the most spectacular in Belgium. For the millennium New Year's celebration, Brussels turned the entire Grand' Place into one big ballroom. Music, dancing, and celebrating were enjoyed in the open air under what was billed as "the biggest chandelier in the world," a beautiful, ornate outdoor chandelier hung with six large glowing lanterns and hundreds of tiny lights.

Best wishes for the new year

Following the old French custom, some families in Wallonia wait until New Year's Day to exchange presents. Now is the proper day for Père Noël to arrive, sometimes accompanied by *Père Fouettard*, whose name, meaning Father Spanker, tells you all you need to know about him!

Early on New Year's Day, children in villages throughout Belgium travel from house to house, singing traditional songs welcoming the new year and wishing the residents of the house health and happiness in the months to come. They are rewarded for their performances with cookies and candy and an orange.

According to old French customs, some families, particularly in Wallonia, exchange presents on New Year's Day rather than Christmas Day.

On New Year's Day, children are front and center everywhere in Belgium. Now is their chance to read aloud the letters they have written to their parents and grandparents. In the late morning, while other members of the family enjoy coffee or hot chocolate and cake, or before the big New Year's dinner, children stand up to read, one by one.

Their letters—written in school, or with the help of parents, for little ones at home—express their love and appreciation for the adults who care for them. There are letters for *lieve ouders* (dear parents), *lieve oma and opa* (dear grandma and grandpa), *lieve meter* (dear godmother), and *lieve peter* (dear godfather). With each letter, the child stands in front of the chosen adult, then bows, reads

A Glass of Christmas Cheer

Beer is a natural part of the celebration of the season. In Brussels, friends meet in an *estaminet* (cozy little beer café) to enjoy a Christmas beer and a stew or *hutsepot* (chunky soup that is a meal in itself), or maybe sausage with cheese.

Once, every Belgian village had a brewery or two of its own. Today, there are far fewer, but those remaining offer over 500 kinds of beer. Nearly 90 special Christmas brews are offered each year. Stella Artois, the most popular Christmas beer, was introduced in 1926. It is now brewed all year. Dobbel Palm is a Christmas beer created in 1947 to celebrate its brewery's 200th anniversary. People celebrate the launch of this sweet, full-bodied brew each November.

Saint Feuillien Brewery describes its Saint Feuillien Cuvée de Noël beer as having a very subtle bitterness and recommends a balloon glass for optimal enjoyment.

A grand *Kerstbierfestival*

Every beer requires a specific glass—a tumbler, a flute, a snifter, a chalice, a trumpet-shaped glass, or a large, short-stemmed, very round goblet.

(Christmas Beer Festival) is held for two days in December. The small parish center of Essen-Statie welcomes about 1,000 people to celebrate and sample Christmas beers, including *Kerstschaap* (Christmas sheep). Some meals are prepared with Christmas beer, and bread is baked with Christmas beer.

Christmas beers tend to be rich, dark ales. Some beers are light, but laced with orange peel or Christmas spices such as cinnamon, allspice, ginger, and nutmeg. These beers are perfect for dark, cold winter days and nights. Gluhkriek, served hot, on draught, is a dark red beer with a taste of cherries and spicy cloves—perfect if you have a sweet tooth. Bush de Noël, the most substantial Christmas beer, is an amber-red colored barley wine with a complex but inviting nose (scent) of raisins, coriander, malt, and something fruity. Bush Millennium, with an alcohol content of 13 percent, warms you like cognac and has a light bitterness. It is like eating and drinking at the same time. Fantôme de Noël is a very dark beer with hints of toffee, coffee, roasted malt, and vanilla pods.

Like other Belgian beers, Christmas beers have charming names and delightful art on their labels. Other offerings include such whimsical names as La Haute de Père Noël, La Mère de Noël, Delirium Noël, Nazareth 2000, Nectar de Noël, Stille Nacht, and Avec Les Bons Voeux.

the letter, and bows again. As a reward, the child is given a little money to put in a savings bank or to buy something he or she would dearly love to have. Even children too young to read follow the ritual, holding the paper their parents helped them write and "reading."

This custom is continued by the adults when they return to work on January 2. Office workers present their best wishes to their supervisors, and the supervisors take their own good wishes to their bosses, and so on up the line.

Off to a lively start

New Year's is the occasion for the polar-bear club of Ostend to strut—or swim—their stuff, taking their traditional dip in the North Sea. Because even watching such a stunt is difficult, free gin and free soup are served on the beach to warm the spirits of spectators. Strolling along the boardwalk there, polar-bear-club fans also can fill up on fried fish snacks—free!

Cold-water swimmers in Bruges get a head start. Just before noon on December 30, the Polar Bears of Bruges take a refreshing swim in the ice-cold waters of the city's canals.

In Ronse, a little town tucked in the hills of the Ardennes, the first week of the new year is the time

Wild and colorful parades like this one are just part of the Bommel Feast and Crazy Monday celebration in Ronse the first week of the new year.

for the Bommel Feast and Crazy Monday celebration. There's a carnival atmosphere in the city all week, with thousands of people arriving from all over Belgium to parade, sing, and dance in the streets as they see the new year in.

Driekoningen celebrations

In Koksijde, children, grown-ups, tourists, and anyone else who wants to join in can take part in the annual New Year's "Star Parade." On January 2, everyone dresses up like one of the Three Wise Men and parades through the streets.

Three Kings Day, January 6, is a good reason for another parade of sorts all around Flanders, *Driekoningen*. In the villages there,

For January celebrations, people dress like the Three Wise Men. Sometimes children dressed in costume walk from house to house singing and collecting money for charity.

children wear a crown on their heads and carry a star on a stick. A little string can be pulled to make the star spin. The children may also dress in fanciful costumes. Then they walk from house to house, knock on the door, and sing traditional Driekoningen songs. Each child carries a box to collect money for charity. The people they entertain put money in each child's box and also give the singers some candy or chocolates, too.

In some areas, particularly around Oudenaarde, grown-ups do a very similar thing. Dressed up and masked, they go from house to house, talking in strange voices to further confuse the friends they visit. They don't want anyone to guess their identities. They aren't looking for money. They simply expect to share a drink with friends and have a little fun making them guess who their visitors are.

Three Kings Day, January 6, is a good reason for another parade of sorts . . .

Now that families move from city to city more often and are not likely to know every family in their village, the game has shifted to cafés. Men and women meet in the cafés on January 6 and have great fun seeing one another in disguise and talking in funny voices, trying to remain mysterious while they identify everyone around them. In Antwerp, the cafés give their costumed patrons a free *worstenbroodje* (sausage pie) with their first beer of the day.

Elsewhere, Belgians celebrate January 6 by sharing a *Driekoningentaart,* a Three Kings pie or cake. One dried pea is baked into the pie. The person who gets the pea in his or her piece of pie receives a present. In bakeries, the special pies are marked with a gold paper crown. The pea recipient puts on the crown and becomes king. Even if the winner is a woman or girl, she is crowned king.

In French regions of the country, January 6 is called the *Fête des rois* (Feast of the Kings). The special cake, called the *galette de rois* (kings' cake), is almond-flavored, and the bean inside is plastic.

Kerstboomverbranding: the fiery finish

Nearly everywhere in the country, *Kerstboomverbranding* is the last hurrah of Christmas in Belgium. *Kerstboomverbranding* means Christmas-tree burning. On January 11 or 12, after all the holiday festivities are over, people add their Christmas trees to the huge pile in the village fire pit—made just for this occasion. In Landen and other towns, the Christmas-tree burning is the culmination of a torchlight parade and the occasion for performances by local artists. Holiday refreshments are served in a heated tent.

This dramatic tradition provides the perfect blazing finale to the Christmas holiday season in Belgium. Pine trees, especially dry pine Christmas trees that have been inside houses bearing ornaments for days—and getting drier every day—burn with an amazingly bright, fierce flame. A pile of Christmas trees creates the perfect blaze to see the old year out.

On Kerstboomverbranding, Belgians burn their Christmas trees together in village fire pits. The brilliant, jumping blazes mark the official end of the holiday season.

Belgian Crafts

Lace Medallion

Display this lace ornament in a place of honor on your tree.

- white or beige cotton lace doily (available at craft stores)
- scissors
- corrugated cardboard square, at least 6 inches by 6 inches (can use recycled scrap cardboard from a carton)
- 8 straight pins
- spray fabric stiffener or spray starch
- ½ yard white or beige pique ribbon (to match doily)
- school glue or hot-glue gun
- monofilament fishing line

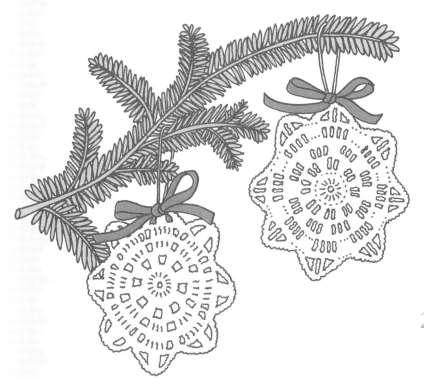

What to Do

1. Cut out an ornamental pattern from the doily. It should be small enough to hang on a tree—about 5 inches maximum. Handle carefully so that the edges do not unravel.

2. Pin the ornamental pattern to the cardboard square. Spray with fabric stiffener or starch.

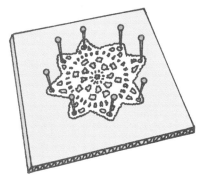

3. When dry, remove pins and carefully lift off the medallion. Use a small dab of glue to attach a ribbon bow to the medallion. Allow to dry.

4. Make a hanger from a loop of monofilament fishing line (knotted at top).

Snow Globe

Some waterproof glues require up to 24 hours to dry, so check package directions before starting this project to make sure you allow enough time to complete it.

Materials

- ✂ clear glass jar with lid, rounded shape if possible (Baby food jars make great snow globes, so do small, rounded condiment jars. Some foods that might come in rounded jars are cocktail onions, maraschino cherries, mustard, honey, and jams and jellies.)
- ✂ small plastic figurine of winter or Christmas design, such as a Nativity scene, snowman, Christmas tree, or ice skater, that is small enough to fit inside jar. You can find small plastic figurines at the craft store, or at a party-goods store; look in party favors section.
- ✂ water
- ✂ glycerin (sold in drug stores)
- ✂ silver or iridescent white glitter
- ✂ waterproof glue

What to Do

1. Soak the jar in warm soapy water to remove the label and any adhesive. Rinse out the jar. Dry it thoroughly. If it still smells like the food that had been stored in it, allow it to air-dry for a few hours.

2. Before gluing, test to be sure figurine fits all the way inside the jar. Glue the figurine to the inside of the jar lid. Allow to dry completely—check directions on glue package to find out how long this will take.

3. Fill the jar ⅔ full with cool water, then add glycerin to fill jar almost to the top. Add a teaspoon or more of glitter, depending on size of jar and how much "snow" you want your scene to have.

4. Glue the lid shut by putting a small amount of glue all the way around the inside edge of the lid. Carefully screw the lid on tight. Allow to dry thoroughly.

5. Turn your globe over, shake, and watch the blizzard!

Christmas Potpourri Bag

Fragrant and pretty, potpourri can be used to decorate and scent any room in the house. If the weather is warm where you live, your own flower garden may be the perfect place to find potpourri materials. Just start your project 10 days in advance so you can pick and dry the petals, buds, and leaves.

- 6 cups of the following, any combination: dried flowers and leaves, pine or other evergreen needles (You can get these from a store selling live Christmas trees—ask if they have any leftover branches from trees that were given a "fresh cut" for customers.), miniature pine cones, cinnamon sticks (broken into small pieces), dried orange peel, whole cloves, bay leaves, dried moss, and cedar chips
- large mixing bowl
- fragrance oil with a wintry scent, such as bayberry, evergreen, cranberry, or cinnamon
- cellophane "goodie bag" (available where party supplies are sold)
- 18 inches of 2-inch lace ribbon

What to Do

1. Place dried flowers and leaves and other ingredients in a large mixing bowl. When choosing the ingredients for your potpourri, try for a variety of colors, shapes, sizes, and textures. A Christmas potpourri might feature lots of red flowers and green leaves and moss. (Reserve half a dozen especially pretty pieces.)

2. Evenly distribute approximately 30 drops of fragrance oil on the assorted flowers, pine cones, and spices. Gently mix to distribute the oils.

3. Fill gift bag ¾ full with potpourri. Gently place the reserved pieces on the top of the potpourri.

4. Tie tightly with lace ribbon. When the scent of the potpourri fades, refresh with a dozen or more drops of the same fragrance oil.

Lacy Snowflakes

Hang snowflakes from the ceiling at varying heights for a "snowstorm" effect. Or, make a centerpiece by hanging lacy snowflakes from tree branches held by a base. Consider spray painting the branches white before hanging the snowflakes on them.

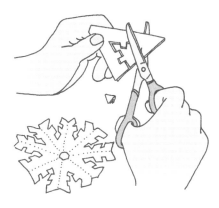

Materials

- several sheets of thick blank white paper
- scissors
- silver or pearly white glitter glue
- monofilament fishing line
- tree branches, spray painted white (optional)

What to Do

1. Diagonally fold over a sheet of paper as shown. Cut off the excess where the halves do not overlap. Unfold the paper. You will now have a perfect square.

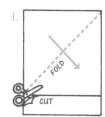 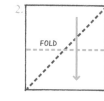 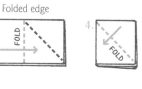

Folded edge

2. Fold the flattened square in half horizontally as shown.

3. Fold the rectangle again as shown.

4. Refold the small square along the existing diagonal line.

5. Use scissors to cut shapes into the sides of the triangle. Be careful not to cut away an entire side along a fold line—leave some folded paper intact. You may cut off the tips of the triangle, but do not cut too deep.

6. Unfold your triangle and see what kind of snowflake you've made. Experiment with other snowflakes to see what forms the most interesting patterns. (Tip: The more paper you cut away, the lacier and more delicate your snowflake will be.)

7. Decorate your snowflake with glitter glue. (Decorate one side, then allow to dry before doing second side.)

8. Hang your snowflakes using monofilament fishing line.

Belgian Carols

Bright December Moon
Zie de maan schijnt

Bright De - cem - ber moon is beam - ing, Boys and girls now stop your
Zie de maan schijnt donr de bo - men, Mak-kers slaakt mo wild ge

play! For to - night's the wondrous evening, Eve of good Saint Nicholas
raas! 't Heerlijk a - voudj is ge ko-men, 't l-mond je van Sin - ter

Day. O'er the roofs his horse un - shod Bring us gifts or else the rod,
klaas. Vol ver wach - ting klopt ons hart, Wie de kock krijgt wie de gard.

O'er the roofs his horse un - shod, Bring us gifts or else the rod.
Vol ver wach-ting klopt ons hart, Wie de kock krijgt wie de gard.

The Simple Birth
De Nederige Geboorte

Andante con moto

1. From Heav'n there came to earth a Ba - by so small: From
1. Er is een kin - de - kin ge - bo - ren op d'aard': Er

Heav'n there came to earth a Ba - by so small:
is een kin - de - kin ge - bo - ren op d'aard':

Je - sus, who came for the sake of us all. _____
't Kwam op de aar - de voor ons al - le - gaar. _____

Je - sus, who came for the sake of us all.
't Kwam op de aar - de voor ons al - le - gaar.

2. Beneath His tiny head no pillow but hay;
   God's richest treasure in rude manger lay.

3. His eyes of blackest jet were sparkling with light,
   Rosy cheeks bloomed on His face fair and bright.

4. And from His lovely mouth, the laughter did swell,
   When He saw Mary, whom He loved so well.

5. He came to weary earth, so dark and so drear,
   To wish to mankind a blessed New Year.

2. Er is een kindekin geboren in 't strooi,
   't Lag in een kribbetje gedekt met hooi.

3. 't Had twee schoon oogjes, zoo zwart als laget,
   Twee bleusende kaakjes, dat stond hem zoo net.

4. 't Keek naar zijn moeder en 't lachte zoo snel,
   't Kende de liefde zijns moeders zoo wel.

5. 't Kwam op de aarde voor ons allegaar,
   En 't wenscht ons een zalig nieuwe jaar.

Belgian Recipes

Belgian Waffles

1 envelope active dry yeast
3 cups warm milk
3 egg yolks
12 tbsp. unsalted butter,
    melted and cooled to room temperature
½ cup granulated sugar
1¼ tsp. salt
2 tsp. vanilla extract
4 cups sifted all-purpose flour
3 egg whites
confectioners' sugar
whipped cream
fresh peach slices or berries (optional)

In a small mixing bowl, whisk together the dry yeast and ¼ cup of the warm milk. Let stand 5 minutes, or until yeast is completely dissolved.

In a large mixing bowl, whisk together the egg yolks, another ¼ cup of the milk, and the melted butter. Add the yeast mixture, along with the sugar, salt, and vanilla; whisk thoroughly. Add the flour and the remaining milk, alternating them; add about 1 cup of the flour and ½ cup of the milk at a time, mixing thoroughly.

In a clean, small mixing bowl, use an electric mixer on medium speed to beat egg whites till soft peaks form. Gently fold egg whites into batter.

Cover bowl with a clean kitchen towel and set in a warm, dry place to rise until doubled in volume (about 1 hour). Stir down the batter.

Preheat waffle iron. Spray with nonstick cooking spray. Ladle ½ cup batter onto waffle iron, spreading with back of a spatula until batter is ¼ inch from edges of waffle iron. Close lid and bake until the waffle is lightly browned. Keep finished waffles warm in single layer in 200 °F oven. Dust with confectioners' sugar and top with whipped cream. Serve with fresh fruit if desired.

Makes one dozen 6-inch waffles.

Piquant Beet Salad

Note: The beets may be prepared up to one week in advance and stored in refrigerator. Stir daily to blend flavors.

5 small beets (about 1½ lbs.)
salt
4 tbsp. vegetable oil
2 tbsp. walnut oil
2 tbsp. fresh lemon juice
⅛ tsp. dried dill

1 small onion, thinly sliced
freshly ground black pepper
4 cups Boston, bibb, or butter lettuce
   leaves, torn into small pieces
2 tbsp. minced chervil or parsley
lemon wedges

Wash and scrub beets; do not peel. Trim green tops down to the inch closest to the beets. Place beets in a medium saucepan and add enough cold water to cover by at least 3 inches. Add ½ tsp. salt. Bring to a boil; reduce heat and simmer till fork-tender (25 to 40 minutes). Drain and cool for 10 minutes.

Peel beets and cut into ½-inch cubes and place in a mixing bowl. Combine vegetable oil, walnut oil, lemon juice, and dill; whisk well. Pour vinaigrette dressing over beets. Add onion slices. Season to taste with salt and pepper. Refrigerate at least 2 hours, stirring often.

To serve, remove beets and onions with slotted spoon. Arrange on lettuce leaves on a serving platter. Spoon some of the leftover dressing over the salad. Garnish with chervil or parsley and lemon wedges.

White Asparagus Soup

1½ lbs. fresh white asparagus
   (can substitute green asparagus)
2 tbsp. unsalted butter
4¼ cups chicken stock
1 medium onion, coarsely chopped
3 cloves garlic, peeled and sliced

½ cup dry white wine
¼ cup heavy cream
1 tsp. salt
⅛ tsp. freshly ground white pepper
chopped fresh parsley

Wash asparagus and trim well, discarding tough ends. Peel any stalks that are not very young and thin. Reserve all tips, and chop remaining stalks into 1-inch pieces. Set aside.

In a soup pot, heat the butter and ¼ cup of the stock over medium heat until butter is melted. Add onion and garlic, cooking until tender but not browned (about 5 minutes). Add remaining chicken stock, white wine, and chopped asparagus. Bring to a boil, then lower heat and simmer for 20 minutes. Puree the soup in a food processor or blender. Return to pot and stir in the cream, salt, pepper, and reserved asparagus tips. Simmer for 5 minutes. Ladle into warmed bowls and sprinkle parsley over top to garnish.

Serves 4.

Flemish Beef Stew

Note: Like most stews, this recipe can be prepared in advance and refrigerated or frozen. It improves with age.

4 lbs. boneless stewing beef (such as chuck,
   short rib meat, or bottom round)
3 tbsp. all-purpose flour
1 tsp. salt
½ tsp. freshly ground black pepper
4 tbsp. unsalted butter
2 lbs. onions, thinly sliced
2 12-oz. bottles dark Belgian or other beer
2 bay leaves
2 sprigs fresh thyme or 1 tsp. dried thyme
¼ tsp. dried marjoram
1 tbsp. cider vinegar
2 tbsp. brown sugar, lightly packed
chopped fresh parsley

Cut beef into 2-inch cubes, trimming excess fat. Mix flour with salt and pepper in a soup bowl. Dredge beef cubes in flour mixture, coating all sides. Brush off excess flour.

In large frying pan, melt 2 tbsp. of the butter over medium heat. Sauté small batches of beef cubes, turning till browned on all sides. Remove with fork or slotted spoon and set aside till all cubes are browned. (Add 1 tbsp. butter if needed partway through sautéing batches.)

Melt remaining butter in frying pan. Sauté onions till lightly browned (about 10 minutes). Combine onions and beef cubes in a Dutch oven.

Pour beer into frying pan to deglaze, scraping with wooden spoon to loosen flavorful brown bits. Bring to a boil, then turn off heat.

Pour the beer over the meat and onions. Add bay leaves, thyme, and marjoram. Bring to a boil, then reduce heat and simmer, covered, till meat is fork-tender (about 2 hours). Remove from heat and skim any fat from surface. Mix in vinegar and brown sugar. Return to heat and simmer for 5 minutes. Serve over hot, buttered egg noodles, or with crispy French bread. Garnish with fresh parsley.

Serves 6.

Bûche de Noël — Christmas Log Cake

Cake

¼ cup sifted cake flour
1 tsp. baking powder
⅛ tsp. salt
¼ cup milk
2 tbsp. unsalted butter
⅛ tsp. vanilla extract
¼ cup sugar
5 eggs

Frosting

2 cups heavy cream
8 oz. semisweet chocolate,
  finely chopped
1 cup sugar
⅔ cup water
¼ tsp. cream of tartar
¼ cup rum
sweetened cocoa powder (optional)

Begin this recipe early in the day one or two days in advance.

Preheat oven to 400 °F. Grease a 17½-inch x 11½-inch jelly roll pan. Cut a piece of waxed paper or parchment paper to fit bottom of pan precisely; lay paper in pan.

Sift together flour, baking powder, and salt four times. Set aside. In small saucepan, heat milk, butter, and vanilla extract over medium heat till butter is melted. Remove from heat.

In large mixing bowl, use handheld electric mixer to beat sugar and eggs together till tripled in volume and the consistency of soft-whipped cream (about 12 minutes). Reheat the butter-and-milk mixture till steaming. In three equal batches, sift the flour-and-baking powder mixture over the egg mixture, folding dry ingredients into wet ones after each batch. Add butter-and-milk mixture; fold in till well mixed. Pour batter into prepared jelly roll pan, scraping bottom of bowl with rubber spatula or wooden spoon. Spread evenly.

Bake till top is golden brown and springs back when lightly pressed with fingertip (about 8 to 10 minutes). Remove from oven. Immediately run butter knife along edges to separate cake from the pan. Quickly invert cake pan onto a sheet of aluminum foil so cake falls out onto foil; tap pan lightly if necessary. Allow cake to cool thoroughly, then peel off paper liner.

Carefully lift foil with cake, and invert over another sheet of foil. Gently peel off the top sheet of foil. (Browned surface of cake will stick to the peeled foil; this is fine.) Set cake aside to prepare frosting.

In medium saucepan, bring cream to a boil. Remove from heat and whisk in chocolate. Cover pan and let stand 10 minutes. Use rubber spatula to stir cream mixture thoroughly, scraping bottom of pan till all chocolate is mixed well. Cover and chill for 3 hours or more. When ready to frost cake, beat frosting with handheld electric mixer on medium speed just till slightly softened but still holding shape. The mixture should still be thick.

In small saucepan, cook sugar, water, and cream of tartar over low heat till most sugar has dissolved; stir gently with wooden spoon as it cooks. Simmer for 2 minutes; do not stir while simmering. Remove from heat and allow to cool thoroughly. Add rum to cooled syrup mixture; mix well.

Use pastry brush to generously spread the syrup-and-rum mixture over top of prepared sponge cake. Spread along with half the chocolate cream. Working from one of the short sides, roll up the cake very tightly. (To roll, fold about 1 inch of cake over filling, then slowly roll, keeping cake even and making sure foil does not stick to it. If cake cracks on first few rolls, do not worry—cracking will lessen as the roll gets wider.) Gently roll over the finished cake roll, if necessary so seam is on bottom. Spread remaining chocolate frosting roughly over the cake, using blade of a serrated steak knife to mimic the texture of tree bark. Refrigerate until 2 hours before serving time. Let cake come to room temperature. If desired, lightly sift sweetened cocoa powder over the cake. Slice with butter knife or other sharp knife.

Serves 12.

⚜

Speculoos

3 cups flour
⅔ cup butter, softened
½ cup dark brown sugar
1 tsp. baking powder
½ tsp. salt
1 tsp. cinnamon
½ tsp. nutmeg
½ tsp. ground cloves
½ cup molasses

Preheat oven to 350 °F. Butter a baking sheet (or spray with cooking spray) and set aside.

Knead all the ingredients together into a soft ball. Roll out on a floured board to a sheet ¼ inch thick. Cut shapes with cookie cutters. Use spatula to transfer cookies to baking sheet. (If you prefer, use a mold to form the cookies. Flour the mold lightly, then roll the dough onto it, pressing into the recessed areas; cut away the excess dough with a sharp knife, then turn mold upside down and tap sharply to unmold cookies onto baking sheet.)

Bake the cookies on the buttered baking sheet for 20 to 25 minutes or until brown. Cool on wire racks.

Makes about 4 to 6 dozen cookies.

Chestnut-Cranberry Stuffing

6 tbsp. unsalted butter
2 cups chopped onions
1 cup chopped celery
¼ cup minced fresh parsley
1½ cups canned or freshly
   baked and peeled chestnuts, chopped
½ cup dried cranberries
¾ tsp. salt
½ tsp. ground black pepper

¼ tsp. nutmeg
⅛ tsp. ground cloves
pinch of rosemary
1 tbsp. fresh grated orange peel
10 cups unseasoned prepared
   bread cubes
½ cup chicken stock
2 eggs, beaten

Preheat oven to 350 °F. Melt butter in large frying pan. Add onions and celery; sauté until tender but not brown (about 5 minutes). Remove from heat.

Stir in parsley, chestnuts, cranberries, spices, and grated orange peel. Toss in bread crumbs. Pour chicken stock and egg over all and mix well. Stuffing mixture should be lightly moist but not clumped together. If dry, add cool water 1 tsp. at a time until moist.

Pour stuffing mixture into a large, shallow baking dish that has been sprayed with cooking spray. Bake in 350 °F oven until stuffing is heated through well and top is lightly brown and has formed a crust (about 25 to 40 minutes). Serve immediately or refrigerate. (Can be made a day in advance and reheated in oven after sprinkling water over top and covering dish with foil.)

Serves 6.

Smitane Sauce

Note: Smitane Sauce is a classic accompaniment for roasted poultry, game birds, and veal.

1¼ cups chicken or vegetable broth
1½ tbsp. unsalted butter
1½ tbsp. all-purpose flour
¼ cup minced white or portabello mushrooms
2 tbsp. unsalted butter

¼ cup minced shallots
1 cup dry white wine
1 cup reduced-fat sour cream
salt
freshly ground white pepper

In small saucepan, heat broth until hot. Cover and set aside. In medium saucepan, melt butter. Stir in flour, whisking well. Cook over low heat, stirring constantly, till mixture is pale tan color (about 5 minutes). Remove from heat and cool for 2 minutes. Whisk in the stock, a little at a time; add mushrooms and stir well. Return pan to stove and bring to a simmer, whisking constantly. Cook over medium-low heat till sauce is thick enough to coat the back of a spoon (about 20 minutes); do not allow to boil. Whisk in 1 tbsp. of the butter. Set aside.

In small saucepan, melt 1 tbsp. butter. Stir in shallots; cook till translucent but not brown. Add white wine. Cook over medium heat till liquid has reduced by half. Gradually stir in the reserved white sauce and simmer 5 minutes. Remove from heat. Stir in sour cream. Season to taste with salt and pepper.

Makes about 2½ cups.

Glossary

aardappel kroketjes (ARD ahp uhl kroh KATZ) fried potato croquettes.

begijnhof (buh GEHN HAHF) a small community of women who lived and worked together in the 1100's and 1200's.

bisque de homard (BIHSK duh ah MAHR) a lobster soup that is a dish of the traditional Christmas dinner in Belgium.

bobbin (BAHB uhn) a reel or spool for holding thread, yarn, and the like. Bobbins are used in machine sewing, spinning, weaving, and lace-making.

boudin (boo DAHNG) pork sausages that are usually boiled in pig blood.

boukètes (boo KATZ) buckwheat crepes (thin pancakes) that have been fried in a pan with butter, raisins, and apple rings, and then sprinkled with brown or white sugar.

boulangere (boo LAHN zhee) a baker.

brioche (BREE awsh) a sweet eggbread or cake with a small ball-shaped dough on top.

Bûche de Noël (BOOSH duh noh EHL) a thin chocolate cake spread with a creamy filling or ice cream, then rolled up into the shape of a log and covered with icing. It's the traditional Christmas dessert in Belgium. Bûche de Noël is also the French traditional burning Christmas log.

commune (KAHM yoon) a city or town in Belgium.

cougnou (koon YOO) a little cake or bread made with raisins and sugar in the shape of the Baby Jesus.

couque du petit Jésus (koo KAY doo puh TEET ZHEH zoo) the town of Ath's version of a cougnou.

dowry (DOW ree) the money or property that a woman brings to her husband when she marries him.

Driekoningen dag (dree KOH nuhng uhn DAKH) the celebration of Three King's Day on January 6.

estaminet (ehs tah mee NEH) a beer café.

glögg (GLUHG) a hearty holiday drink, served hot.

glühwein (GLOO vyn) hot mulled wine.

kenioles (kehn YOHL) a Christmas bread or cake in the province of Hainaut.

Kerstboomverbranding (KARST bohm vuhr BRAND ihng) the Christmas-tree burning celebration held in the village fire pit around January 11 or 12, the last hurrah of the Christmas season in Belgium.

kerstkrans (KARST kranz) green advent wreaths that are hung on doors and over fireplaces during the Christmas season.

kerstman (KARST man) the Flemish name for Santa Claus. The literal meaning is Father Christmas.

marzipan (MAHR zuh pan) a candy made of a paste of ground almonds, egg whites, and sugar.

nonpareils (NAHN puh REHJ) chocolate drops sprinkled with sugar that are used to decorate chocolate wreaths. The decorated wreaths are used as an edible decoration on the Christmas tree.

Père Noël (PAIR noh EHL) Father Christmas or who French-speaking people call Santa Claus.

praline (PRAH leen) French Belgian name for the hard chocolate shell with a cream filling. These Belgian chocolates are known worldwide.

Rond de Cougnole (RAH duh koon YOHL) a terra cotta decoration that is put in the center of cougnous.

santons (sahn TAWN) small figurines representing the Baby Jesus and all the people and animals present at the first Christmas. Santons are put in the Nativity scenes.

Saint Nikolas (SAYNT nihk LAHS) Saint Nicholas. The patron saint of children. He is also Belgium's main gift giver.

speculoos (spay kyoo LAHS) a popular Belgian spice cookie that is baked in homes and bakeries during the Christmas season. Children put these out for Saint Nicholas on December 5, Saint Nicholas Eve.

trairies (tra REE) a traditional card game that is played in Belgian cafes and bakeries after Midnight Mass.

Index

Page numbers in italic type refer to illustrations alone.

Acknowledgments

Cover	© Domelounksen, Eureka Slide; © Joe Viesti, Viesti Collection, Inc.
2	© Isopress from Getty Images
5	© Domelounksen, Eureka Slide
6	© Brison, Eureka Slide
9	© Domelounksen, Eureka Slide
10	© David Martyn Hughes, Travel Ink
13	© Michel Damanet, Reporters Press Agency; © Comstock
15	© Eka, Eureka Slide
16	© De Leo, Eureka Slide; © Eka, Eureka Slide
17	Brugge Tourist Office
18	© Ken Gibson, Travel Ink; © M. Merne, Eureka Slide
20	© Wang Mo, Eureka Slide
21	Jeff Guerrant*
22	© Isopress from Getty Images
24	Belgian National Tourist Office; Antwerp Tourist Office
25	© Isopress from Getty Images
26	Belgian National Tourist Office; © Domelounksen, Eureka Slide
29	© Antwerp Tourist Office
30	Belgian Tourist Office; Flanders Tourist Office
31	Antwerp Tourist Office
33	Park Midden Limburg-Bokrijk
34	The Bridgeman Art Library
36	Belgian National Tourist Office
37	© Thomas Vanhaute, Panos Pictures
38	© Eka, Eureka Slide
39	© Domelounksen, Eureka Slide
40	© Alain Schroeder, Reporters Press Agency
43	© Eka, Eureka Slide
44	Imperial War Museum
46	Belgian National Tourist Office
48	© Eka, Eureka Slide
51	© StockFood America
53	© Eka, Eureka Slide; © PhotoDisc, Inc.
54	© De Fraigne, Eureka Slide
56-57	© Dick Caremans, Hippofoto
58	© V. D. Branden, Eureka Slide
59	© Verpoorten, Reporters Press Agency
60	© Belgian National Tourist Office
61	Ronse Tourist Office
62	Belgian National Tourist Office
64	Antwerp Tourist Office

Craft Illustrations: Eileen Mueller Neill and Kimberly Neill*

Recipe Cards: World Book photos by Dale DeBolt*

Advent Calendar: © PhotoDisc, Inc.

Advent Calendar Illustrations: Eileen Mueller Neill*

All entries marked with an asterisk (*) denote illustrations created exclusively for World Book, Inc.